Smithsonian

CURIOUS ABOUT PLUTO

JUN 14 2016

by James Buckley Jr.

GROSSET & DUNLAP

An Imprint of Penguin Random House

GROSSET & DUNLAP

Penguin Young Readers Group
An Imprint of Penguin Random House LLC

Smithsonian

This trademark is owned by the Smithsonian Institution and is registered in the U.S. Patent and Trademark Office.

Smithsonian Enterprises:
Christopher Liedel, President
Carol LeBlanc, Senior Vice President, Education and Consumer Products
Brigid Ferraro, Vice President, Education and Consumer Products
Ellen Nanney, Licensing Manager
Kealy Gordon, Product Development Manager

Smithsonian National Air and Space Museum:
Andrew K. Johnston, Geographer, Center for Earth and Planetary Studies

- -

PHOTO CREDITS: NASA: back cover (bottom), 6 (bottom), 7 (right), 8 & 15 (photos by Bill Ingalls), 10. **NASA/APL/SWRI:** front cover, 1, 18, 19, 22. **NASA/JHUAPL/SWRI:** back cover (top), 1, 4, 5, 7 (left), 12, 13, 14, 16, 17, 23, 24, 25, 26, 27, 28, 29, 31, 32. **NASA/LASP:** 17 (bottom). **SMITHSONIAN NATIONAL AIR AND SPACE MUSEUM:** 11. **THINKSTOCK:** 2–3 (photo by standret), 9 (photo by pablofdezr). The labels on some charts have been simplified for reading level.

- -

Library of Congress Cataloging-in-Publication Data is available.

ISBN 978-0-399-54218-3   10 9 8 7 6 5 4 3 2 1

Did you ever look up
at night and think,

"What's out there?

What's really,

really, *really*

far out there?"

In July 2015, we got a good look at something far out in our solar system:

PLUTO!

Scientists used computers to make the colors easier to see in this photo of Pluto. The colors show differences in its surface.

A spacecraft called New Horizons was launched on January 19, 2006. It was sent by NASA, the US agency in charge of exploring space. The spacecraft's mission? To photograph Pluto and other objects at the edge of our solar system.

For more than nine years, New Horizons has been whizzing through the solar system. It sped past the moon and past Jupiter in 2007 on its way to Pluto.

New Horizons weighs 1,060 pounds.

Workers on Earth prepared New Horizons for its long trip.

Blast off!

New Horizons was loaded onto an Atlas V rocket.

By July 2015, the New Horizons team was waiting for a message from even farther away. The spacecraft was set to fly by Pluto!

at mission control in Maryland, waiting for a message from Pluto

Pluto is more than three *billion* miles away from the sun. That's almost 40 times the distance between Earth and the sun. Pluto orbits or goes around the sun once every 248 years. It is smaller than our moon.

You could put 150 Plutos inside one Earth!

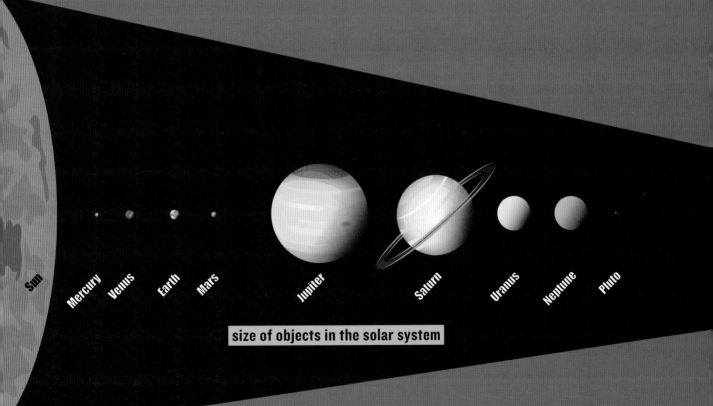

Sun Mercury Venus Earth Mars Jupiter Saturn Uranus Neptune Pluto

size of objects in the solar system

Pluto is in an area in space called the Kuiper (say: KY-per) Belt. The Kuiper Belt is shaped like a doughnut—a giant doughnut around our sun, beyond the planet Neptune. It is filled with many, many icy objects and comets.

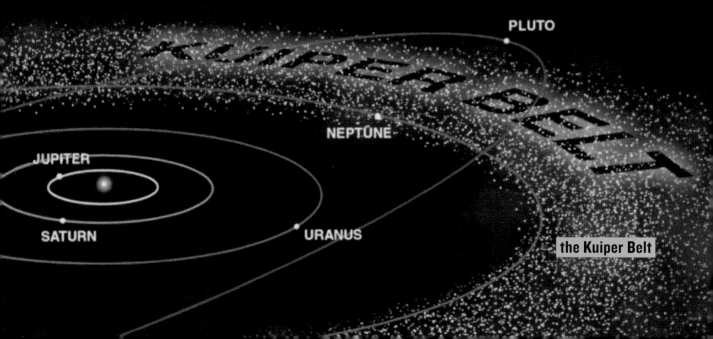

the Kuiper Belt

Pluto was discovered in 1930, when American Clyde W. Tombaugh became the first person to "see" it. Tombaugh used a telescope that also took photographs of the night sky. This helped him see there was a moving object beyond Neptune at the edge of the solar system.

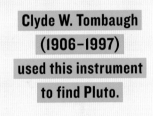

Clyde W. Tombaugh (1906–1997) used this instrument to find Pluto.

This orbiting body needed a name. Tombaugh chose one that came to him from Venetia Burney, an 11-year-old girl from England. She liked Greek and Roman myths and had studied the planets in school. Venetia suggested Pluto, after the Roman god.

Scientists have been able to take close-up pictures of many objects and areas in the solar system. But the Kuiper Belt was difficult to photograph, because it is far away. Pictures of Pluto were tiny and very fuzzy.

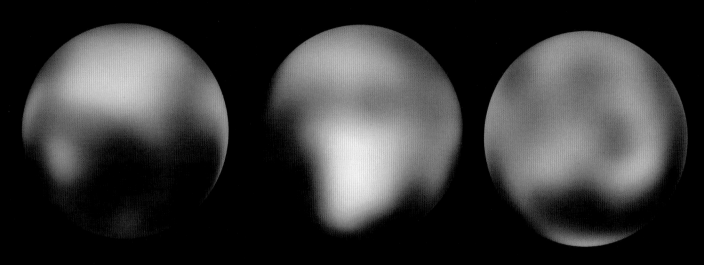

These fuzzy photos of Pluto were taken by the Hubble Space Telescope in February 2010.

New Horizons changed that. It was headed for Pluto—but it would be a long, tricky trip!

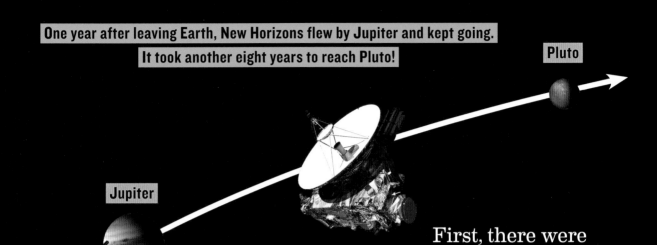

One year after leaving Earth, New Horizons flew by Jupiter and kept going. It took another eight years to reach Pluto!

Pluto

Jupiter

Earth

First, there were those billion of miles to travel. At any point, a tiny pebble slamming into the spacecraft would wreck it. New Horizons would then be stranded millions of miles from home.

Scientists also had to calculate exactly when the moving spacecraft would be near Pluto, which was also moving.

New Horizons would only have three minutes to take good pictures!

Alice Bowman, the New Horizons MOM (missions operations manager) was one of the people waiting for the news. Many women worked on the Pluto mission.

On July 14, 2015, New Horizons was supposed to report that it had reached Pluto. Scientists tracked the spacecraft from mission control in Maryland. They were nervous. Would its signal make it all the way to Earth?

That night the message came through. New Horizons had made it! The first ever flyby of Pluto was a success!

Pluto is so far away, it took the message from New Horizons over four hours to reach mission control. They were happy to get it!

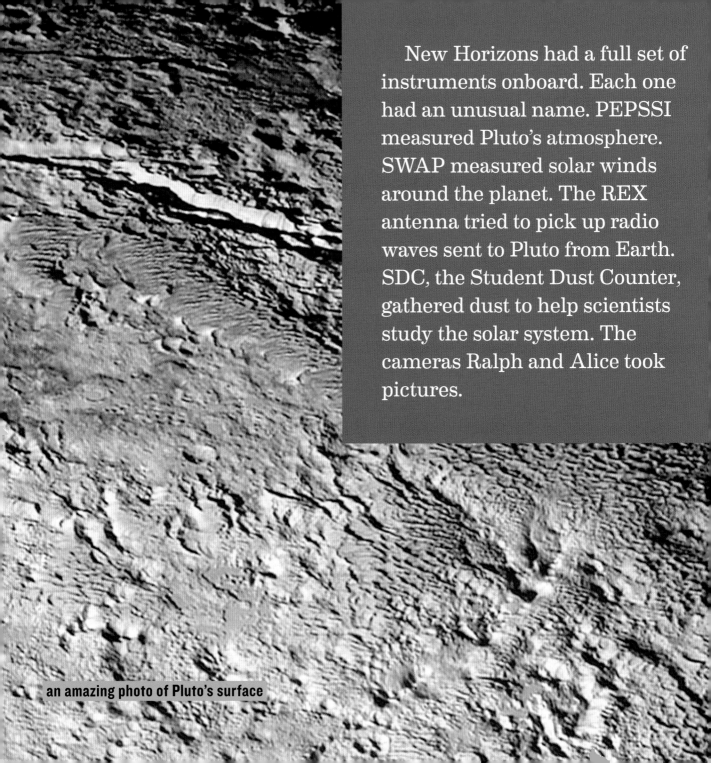

New Horizons had a full set of instruments onboard. Each one had an unusual name. PEPSSI measured Pluto's atmosphere. SWAP measured solar winds around the planet. The REX antenna tried to pick up radio waves sent to Pluto from Earth. SDC, the Student Dust Counter, gathered dust to help scientists study the solar system. The cameras Ralph and Alice took pictures.

an amazing photo of Pluto's surface

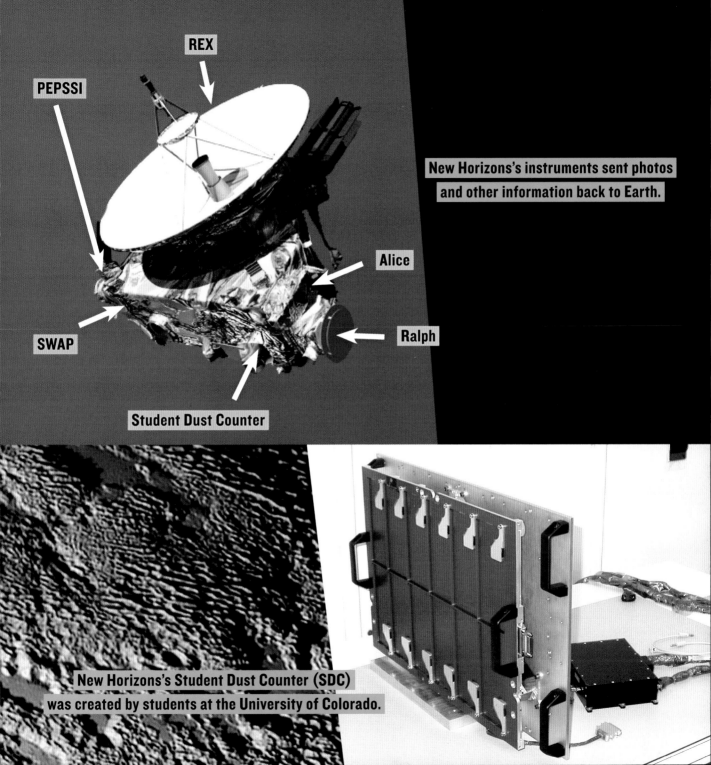

REX

PEPSSI

SWAP

Alice

Ralph

Student Dust Counter

New Horizons's instruments sent photos and other information back to Earth.

New Horizons's Student Dust Counter (SDC) was created by students at the University of Colorado.

Several images showed a wide, flat area on Pluto. It looked like a heart. Scientists named this area after Clyde Tombaugh, the man who first spotted Pluto. Many people texted or tweeted "I ♥ Pluto" when they saw the photos online!

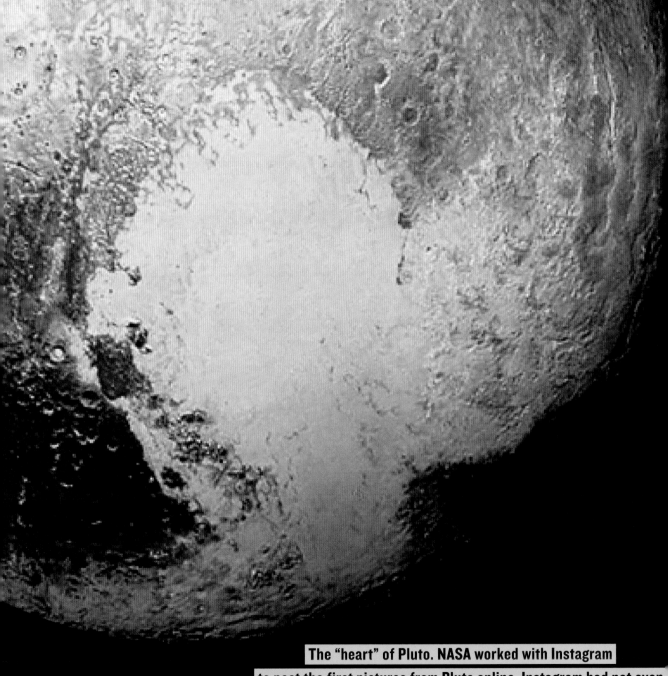

The "heart" of Pluto. NASA worked with Instagram to post the first pictures from Pluto online. Instagram had not even been invented when New Horizons launched in 2006!

During its brief flyby of
Pluto, New Horizons took
hundreds of photos. There were
special cameras on the spacecraft.
There was also a radio that beamed
those pictures across billions of
miles to Earth. Even moving at
the speed of light, the pictures
took hours to reach Earth.

But they were 1,000 times better than any other photos ever taken of Pluto.

People on Earth had never seen Pluto so close up!

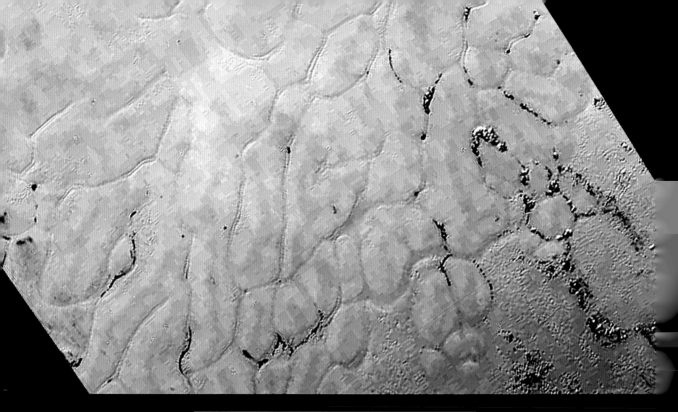

a close-up of an area on **Pluto** with no craters

Scientists were surprised by some things they saw in the photos. There were huge smooth areas with no craters. Craters help scientists figure out how old Pluto might be. They form when something falls on the surface. Older areas are covered with craters. Smooth areas might be much younger.

Scientists also saw big mountains. They rose more than 11,000 feet (3,350 m) above the surface of Pluto.

These mountains on Pluto are taller than the Rocky Mountains in North America!

Pluto is far from the warmth of the sun. So scientists thought they would see a lot of ice there, but they didn't know for sure. The New Horizon photos proved them right.

ice flow edges

The images beamed back showed that Pluto was covered entirely in ice. Some of that ice might still be moving! It appears that sheets of ice have moved across Pluto's surface like glaciers move on Earth.

Scientists were amazed that so much is still happening on Pluto's surface. Some of its ice sheets might be only 100 million years old. That would make them some of the *youngest* areas on any planet in the solar system. (The solar system is more than four *billion* years old!)

Pluto and its moon Charon

New Horizons also sent information about Charon, one of Pluto's moons.

Scientists saw that there was an enormous canyon cutting through Charon's surface. It is about 1,000 miles (1,600 km) long and about 2 miles (3 km) deep. Earth's Grand Canyon is only about a mile deep.

Scientists don't yet know what's in Charon's dark spot.

Photos also show a huge dark area at the northern end of Charon. Scientists named this spot Mordor. That is the name of a dark land in the popular *Lord of the Rings* books and movies.

The spacecraft traveled for more than nine years at a speed of a million miles a day to get close to Pluto. And in just three minutes it had flown past it!

As New Horizons whizzed by, it took "farewell" photos. These amazing pictures show the side of Pluto that does not face the sun. They also clearly show that Pluto has an atmosphere.

Before they saw these pictures, scientists did not think Pluto was warm enough to hold gases.

In its short visit, New Horizons changed what we know about Pluto. It was like meeting a new member of the solar-system family!

And there's much more to come. New Horizons will keep flying, beaming thousands of images back to Earth. Scientists will be studying the photographs and information the spacecraft gathers for years.

In the meantime, New Horizons is still zooming through the Kuiper Belt and deep space.

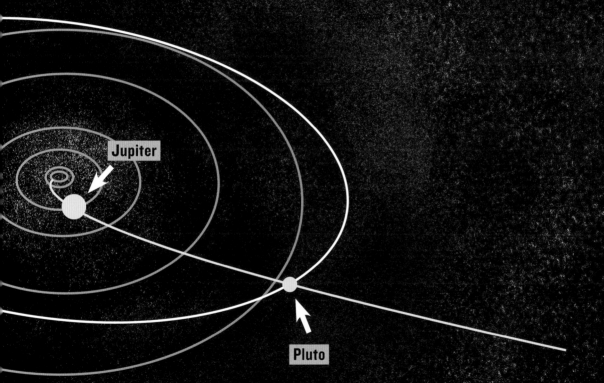

Jupiter

Pluto

Next stop:
out there!

GLOSSARY

astronomer: a person who studies objects in space

atmosphere: the gases that surround a planet

calculate: to use math and numbers to find answers to problems

canyon: a deep cut into the surface of a planet

craters: bowl-shaped indents caused by impacts on a surface

Kuiper Belt: an enormous ring of icy objects orbiting more than three billion miles from the sun

orbits: the paths that planets take around a star, or a moon takes around a planet

solar: having to do with the sun

solar system: our sun and the objects that orbit it

spacecraft: machines that travel in space

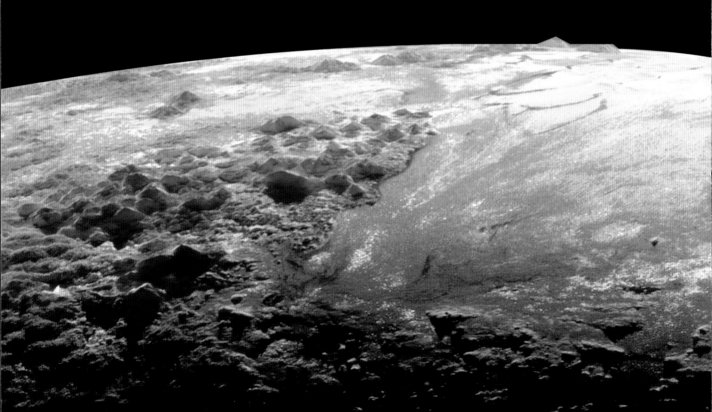